Lambflesh

Lambflesh

Poems by

Caroline Shea

© 2019 Caroline Shea. All rights reserved.
This material may not be reproduced in any form, published,
reprinted, recorded, performed, broadcast,
rewritten or redistributed without
the explicit permission of Caroline Shea.
All such actions are strictly prohibited by law.

Cover design by Shay Culligan
Cover art by Emily Imka

ISBN: 978-1-950462-16-2

Kelsay Books Inc.

kelsaybooks.com

502 S 1040 E, A119
American Fork, Utah 84003

Acknowledgments

All my thanks and gratitude to the journals where the following poems were previously published, often in earlier forms. Your support and belief in my work meant—and means—the world.

Bad Pony Magazine: "Crushed Peaches."

COG Magazine: "Communion."

Crab Fat Magazine: "Diagnostic Notes on *The Bachelorette*."

deluge Literary Journal: "Her."

Dulcet Quarterly: "Hagiography of Wicked Women."

Pankhearst: "Lambflesh."

The Pinch: "Unhooked," and "Post-Surgical Ode."

Poached Hare: "Lineage," and "Backstroke with Lightning."

Shakespeare & Punk: "Devotional for Difficult Girls."

Souvenir: A Journal: "On Asking for Directions Home."

Tinderbox Poetry Journal: "After Seeing Black Swan at Fifteen."

Virga Magazine: "Voicemail with Shipwreck."

I also owe an enormous debt to the authors
who influenced these poems.

~

The poem "Devotional for Difficult Girls," borrows a line from Morgan Parker's *There Are More Beautiful Things Than Beyonce:* "I am getting harder to love each day."

The poem "Un-Mother" is a Golden Shovel, a form created by Terrance Hayes, and is structured around a line by Gwendolyn Brooks: "In the voices of the wind, I hear the voices of my dim killed children."

The italicized line in "Lobotomy Suite," is from Riz Mical's *The Lobotomy Letters: the making of American psychosurgery.* University of Rochester Press; 2013.

The anaphora in "Variations on Nightmare with Intruder," was inspired by Joy Harjo's collection *She Had Some Horses.*

"How to Honeymoon in a Glass House," took inspiration from Anne Carson's "The Glass Essay," particularly in the formal elements of the poem.

In "Unmaking," the line "I am more wonder than fear / these days, but still partly girl," is paraphrased from Georgia O'Keefe's letters to her lover Alfred Stieglitz.

Epigraphs were used including lines from Alison Prine, Charles Simic, and the National Vital Statistics System.

To those have supported me personally and professionally, I truly, for once, do not have the words to express my gratitude.

To my family and friends—Thank you for believing in my words before I did. You have helped me build a life I love. Wherever you are, this is for you.

To my mentors—Thank you for your guidance and compassion. You have shown me how abundant, challenging, and joyful a life anchored in writing can be. Thank you for pushing me to share my work, even when it scared me.

To Max—You know which poems are for you.

Contents

Devotional for Difficult Girls	13
Creation Myth	14
Unhooked	15
Lineage	17
Hellbine:Lovevine	18
Swimming Lessons	19
Un-Mother	20
Viscera	21
Surgical Suite	22
Vitals	23
Lobotomy Suite	24
Hagiography of Wicked Women	26
Variations on Nightmare with Intruder	27
Reporting	29
Excavation, Two Years Later	30
After Seeing *Black Swan* at Fifteen	33
Her	34
Post-Surgical Ode	35
Diagnostic Notes on *The Bachelorette*	36
How to Honeymoon in a Glass House	38
On Asking for Directions Home	40
Backstroke with Lightning	42
Aubade for Vermont with Concussion	43
Unmaking	44
Crushed Peaches	46
Interrogation After Flooding in Ellicot City	47
On Self-Preservation	48
Casualty	49
Meditations on Disaster	51

Voicemail with Shipwreck   53
The Last Known Living Speaker's Survival
    Manual   54
Communion   55
Lambflesh   56

Devotional for Difficult Girls

    after Morgan Parker

I was born an apostle of belief,
a thieved pair of ribs straining in my belly.
I mugged Adam on my way out of the womb
and he's been down-and-out
ever since. *I am getting harder*
to love each day.
In church, I would lie lengthwise
in the pew until the light blurred to dandelion dust
and the ark of the ceiling swayed.
Grant me a body to survive a flood in, Lord.
Something rough and pretty and expensive.
Something untouchable.
If I cry, will you acquit me of my sins?
I forget to brush my teeth too often and am ruinous
in the body you gave me, careless with its meat.
Crack the walnut husk of me open and pick at the goo.
Diagram the fault lines. I calve into such predictable crevasses.
I think I am asking you permission
to exist the way I do.

Creation Myth

A halved fruit, spitting stone. A farm county storm that splits
the sky. And strung through epidural haze:
        white coats, wires, afterbirth.
 I was a worry of a child, a woman, now,
  still damselling my mother's nightmares. I wake from her dreams,

infant skin regrown, jaundiced and thin as papyrus.
How to shed the myth without dismissing the ragged gift
of her love? She hemorrhages
and I swallow the pulp until my stomach swells, her heartbeat
        kicking inside me.

She keeps an old photo of me in the desk drawer—
before breast, before blood, before hardware screwed to bone
        and cratered my skin to moon—
I am three, maybe four, stark naked except for a baseball cap.
I once hated the photo, would wrinkle my nose, embarrassed.
        But this was my body before I knew it was a body,
when I drew my hair a different color each day and believed,
        like most children, I would get what I wanted.

Unhooked

They made a playground game of it—the stretch and snap
        of bra strap striking skin, sweet music of our spandex-ed
                flesh singing. One dove for me, caught only a fist

of cotton shirt, confused. Then snickers. Me, the runt they crowed
        over, a body with nothing worth claiming. This revelation
                of my lack stung more, the taut sheet of my torso

so publicly assessed. Tadpole me shivered shame
        in the locker room the next day, a tissue-thin bralette
                hooked over flatness. I snuck glances

at the other girls, cocooned in matching sets, wondering
        who the hearts drawn on our asses were for.
                To clothe the risk of a budding body in cartoon

and Fruit of the Loom, or to give us some choice
        in how we were viewed, as each pubescent form
                arced away from the years where safety

was presumed? Later, when a boy I'd known since sandboxes
        asked me to be his, I could think only of his anger,
                the time he threw a desk across the room

and was missing from our ranks for several days.
        I scrubbed away my stolen eyeshadow,
                gold streaking in bright fissures down my cheeks.

I learned then to unravel the blood-bright skein of me,
　　　to slip my skin like silk, leaving the self in dark clots
　　　　　across the floor. This is not about blame,

but memory, the way some birds will mimic the call of another,
　　　will learn to milk the usefulness of desire,
　　　　　becoming, for a moment, something else.

Lineage

I don't want
to wake you, so I breathe around
the ache. The first cold week of the year
curdles in my chest. I am so good
at making space for the body's inconveniences.
The ones we carve into the rind
of each day and the ones which carve
themselves into us. There are moments,
looking at the muss of your hair,
where I think tenderness might be worth it.
How do I have to hurt for it to matter?
I have been asking this question
since the bluish bruise of me crested
into the unasked for earth.
Our bodies, the summit
of someone else's desire.
Little lineages of lust and hope.
Some days it seems almost silly—
to want to own oneself.
My silence grows fertile and limp.
In the morning, I will bury
it by the dumpster. Bleary-eyed,
you ask me what the time is.
Speech breaks through shell and membrane,
slips like yolk through my lips.
You know me by the inch,
this flesh and mess of me.
I imagine my *other* body: a divine machine.
I do not think I would know my form unmarked.
And now—the thought uncoils—I do not want to.

Hellbine:Lovevine

Strange daughters, those touch-starved
plants that skew vampiric. But who hasn't
put out roots in another? I know I have,
all wanton and wanting. And maybe this
is what love is, then—playing host to each other
when and how we can. But what of the monstrous
untalked hours? The vein of meanness
streaking though me slick and hot? Some days
my mother sees her mother in my panting
and I redraw myself in the fogged glass.
I still come out crooked. In my last spring up North,
I finally found the campus greenhouse
—cycad, conifer, maidenhair—
a spit of green against snow still souring the outside soil.
I kept a houseplant alive through April, this year,
and it felt like something worth celebrating.
Maybe that will be my offspring: What I choose to nurture.
What growth I leave behind. A dodder vine, spreading,
won't solely strangle its host. Because of this, I am careful
with infection. I tend its infant screams. Soothe it with salt
and hum. Some days I see myself in the bow of my mother's jaw,
stretched taut and quivering. I want to tell her she has tended
what's verdant in me, promise my life will be nothing
but sun and satisfaction. But I don't know what bloom or blight
will make a home in me. And I am too late, too hers, to be
                the answer she needs.

Swimming Lessons

I took to water lapsing-ly,
learning to swim in awkward spurts, a fumbling
pilot of my own form. Yet I craved the lick of salt
or chlorine. The tug and silken hug of it.
Even bathwater thrilled. I soaked until
my toes pruned red and purple, then blanched white.
But I floundered, lacked the breath to stay afloat.
Froze trembling when asked to demonstrate
a simple stroke. Skipped the swim test for years,
lurking in the shallows, while the more buoyant,
the more daring, sliced through air in bright contortions.
In the ocean, oddly most at home, until hooked
by the tide and tumbled under, groundless.
I needed the grit of sand beneath my feet, that pushing off,
so much like dance I'd point my feet beneath the skirt
of each wave, flying. When I still bent daily to the barre,
I hoped to make something beautiful of myself.
Now, I think I have, though instead of beauty, I name it
relief. Name it release. The water cracking like a plate, then
air again   and breath.

Un-Mother

an interrupted Golden Shovel after Gwendolyn Brooks

So much depends on the accident of birth (I
know this). Cleft palate. Club foot. I have
so much to be thankful for. I heard

      of a woman dunked in the Dead Sea, head first, in
      her father's arms. He hoped it would cure the
      palsy. I cannot fault him for this. Our voices

bend towards light like crooked trees. What fingers of
pain are legible, we form into sentences. The
rest of it? It pulls the breath from the body like sudden wind.

      The catalog of my remedies is the
      catalog of my failures. Victorians believed the stoic voices
      of their doctors—with strengthening, the warped bones of

a child could be straightened. And what of my
strength? My moonlit exercises, sit-ups by the dim
blue light of an alarm clock. I have never killed

      or given birth. When I think of the children
      I could bear, I think of their dirty blond hair.
      I wonder what bodies I will bequeath them.

Viscera

My lack a twin, curdling in my stomach.
Watch as it scissors away from my side, arc of everything missing.
It curls around my thumb, nail erupting
from puckered smile of scar, the remnants
of an extra digit. Whistles through my ribcage, one side blank
        as bone. And then a seam of skin stitched
neatly down my spine, slick as a Sunday morning, only missing
the ellipsis of satin buttons. I vomit silk magician's scarves,
perfume the wounds with vanilla and tobacco, press flowers
        between my teeth. I make myself habitable.
Unstitch me and wear me as a pelt, a blood-and-guts ball gown.
Watch as the mirror doppelgangers us into infinity. Tomorrow &
tomorrow & tomorrow. Once a surgeon cringed at the ridge of skin
on my hand, asked if I wanted a neater scar. When has this ever
been about beauty? Just about the viscera of our bodies
spun outwards, the lovely machinery of our lives
        humming the horizon raw.

Surgical Suite

I.

summer opens like a sore, sticky fester of crushed lilac
and pavement baking. i seep through bandages. stain rental sheets
pale yellow. pucker stitch through silk, ends blooming blister,
fraying into puss. this leaky vessel confesses itself
again & again.   a useless criminal.   when starved,
the body scavenges adipose and muscle. somewhere, moths
fall in sheets like snow. there is a room where i am always
eight years old. i want to find that child-self and eat her
                        bones & all.

II.

this is a false body. a ruse. period
blood always smells sweet-rotten
in the summer. strawberries blackening,
sticking in strings to my fingers.
not a body but an aperture:
a tear.   a gap.   a waiting-
to-be-filled. the future spills out
taffeta-skirted. a Sears family photo.
for years, i never smiled with teeth.
just pressed my lips together:
a secret.   a sepal.   a stamen.
a stuttering. soon, the stubborn architecture
my cells have scaffolded seven years will
unscrew.   dislodge.   undo.
in the sink, dishes sit unwashed,
sticky with strawberry guts. the bandages
remain unchanged.

Vitals

Again, piss-less and clammy as a still life. All Dutch half-light
and flies buzzing just out of frame. There are worse places to be.

I have to admit (Don't I?) that there's an appeal. There's a button
for everything here. A shift of the fingertip and someone appears

to sponge my parched mouth. At least Jesus' tongue was wet
with wine. They split my pelt across and now I gaze

with taxidermied eyes. Air thick and honeyed in the throat,
breathlessness vindicates. Here, I must let the body

do its slow-stitched work. Here, I am as heavy as God.
And almost as bloody. If there is supposed to be a lesson,

I haven't learned it. The second time they gurneyed me,
I emerged a gutted wreck, ribs straining skin

like flesh against latex. They planted a forest in me
and it swallowed every inch. The body is a room with no exit.

You can only go in and in.
This is a place governed by need and machine.

Firecrackers light down my spine,
crawl through my ribs to settle like ash in the stomach.

I drag my lawless heart hiccupping forward. A woman
wipes rust from my chin with a cold cloth and feeds me sleep

through an IV. There are worse places to be
than in the body. Until it's your body. Until it's not.

Lobotomy Suite

1.

From: *to cut, to slice. Greek.* Blood-drilled and malarial. My end in any other era. Freeman tested on grapefruits and cadavers—an ice pick to the eye and then tap, tap, tap.

2.

For the whole of a winter, pills meant to soothe addle me antic and hellfire, heckle me into the street at 3 AM in a velvet slip and heels, yelling *come and get me.* I lose entire hours of my life, am left with only the word "hunted."

3.

I hive and swell for Rosemary, her tongue sharped for blunting. And declared "cured." Docile, dotty, doting, de-clawed. So many they ripen me with lineage, score me with their thousands.

4.

I tell the doctor the pills work fine. Each failure to be fixed a mark against me.

5.

Of Patient A, Freeman writes: *a satisfactory patient with the personality of an oyster.* She pours him coffee over and over, forgetting his name each time.

6.

I call the hotline, humid-sick and sleepless, convinced I am leaking poison.

7.

$25 dollars a pop and you can take yours home, too, shiny and new for molding. And how many times have I wished to be putty in the hands that held me? Wished to be an easier thing to hold? Please don't ask me to count.

8.

Here, numbers: 20,000 (ice picks, brains). 4 (the youngest's age).

Hagiography of Wicked Women

I carry with me
only the requisite courage
and a personal hagiography—
psalm of the women before me, sick and angry.
Anthem as refusal of erasure.

The buoyancy of June—peeled from the thick pelt of winter—
rustle of skin and air uninterrupted, intimate.
Summer is slick with possibility and sweat.
Dirt-crusted band-aids on the edge of the bathtub
like scavenged relics. Not the wound,
but the memory of it. Season of razor-nicked kneecaps
and feet tanned leather-tough.

Stasis swamps and suffocates. I cannot live in the lull.
I need the bustle of town, the half-baked crusade of days
bursting with *being*. The best cure
has always been the work of living. Work that risks injury
by definition. So many women saved from themselves—
straitjacketed, silenced, second-fiddled.
I am made and remade by my own hands.
Days daisy-chain across the calendar
and a bumper sticker blares: "WICKED WOMAN
SAVED BY GRACE," and I think how happy,
how blessed, are the unsaved.

Variations on Nightmare with Intruder

after Joy Harjo

I thought I woke up   tucked into bed like an arm
in a sleeve. Linen stretched taut as a straitjacket.
The darkness pocked with glow. The night a symphony
of machines.

I thought I woke up   much later, then. His hand
down my waistband, writhing. Taste of vomit and razor wire
rotting in my cheek. I didn't want it but
I didn't stop it, either.

I thought I woke up   underwater. Submarine chatter breaking
through me like birdsong. They'd left cartoons on.
The Proud Family beckoning, inviting me to rest my fists
on my hips and laugh along. But my hands betrayed:
numb blue blocks of want and no one there to howl it to.

I thought I woke up   months ago
and was clean. It was just the taste of anesthesia
hissing on my tongue.

I thought I woke up   with an unfamiliar arm
heavy around my waist like a gurney strap.
Scrubbed until my body was a bee sting.
Until all the blood had funneled
down the drain.

I thought I woke up   unscarred and living
in a shape that could hold me.
But my hands were steadiest
splitting my own flesh
to suck the nectar from its root. That pain was mine
to summon, falconing back when I craved its talons.

This is different—Awake,
floating heavy-light in the murk of August.
The scar, long healed, busts open.
I am here for the picking.

Reporting

Blood-buzzed and half-asleep as his body muscles in,
the cord and rope of him presses against me unquestioned.
I have an animal's instinct for warmth. His flesh grows hard
along my thigh. Once, I saw a rabbit gut-shot on the pavement—
a perfect ruby of wound. I want to believe she sought shelter,
but can't. I did not think myself worth protecting, then.

Excavation, Two Years Later

That crush of light
    each morning dribbled over
        the white lip of the window ledge.

Pool of me. Sweat and last night's makeup
    skunked around each eye-
        lid, fluttering, squinting into

wakefulness, that tapestry of sky and skin
    and stale water swilled to slice through after-
        taste of gin.

Days plush and idle, swollen with want.
    I dreamt my lips kissed, looped sappy
        songs through speakers on repeat.

Each night the wide stretch of possible
    intoxication, giddy with the snap
        of nickname, the jostle

of our conversation, an intimate flush
    against the skin: this belonging. And with it
        the desire for something else. To be consumed

yet unaltered. To own my own surrender.
    And yes, touch-starved, I wanted proof
        of my body's purpose. I'll admit that.

Wanted to be filled and filling. To satisfy some need
    other than my own unanswerable pulse, crowing.
        When he crawled into my bed,

I thought: *Maybe this is what it is
   to be desired.* Somewhere, you were awake, too,
      working on the car, wearing holes in your shorts.

At first, he only feigned sleep. But he came back and always
   after he heard my blood hum its dumb mistake,
      liquor blooming on my breath. Did I serve

my meat for slaughter? Set the table? My body,
   like a bar fight, screaming hurt me, hurt me, hurt me.
      I believed so, at least for a while.

And when his presence had been scrubbed from skin,
   from kitchen tile, from Facebook profile, when we sold
      his shit and drank champagne from the bottle

to celebrate his being-gone, I knew, stubbornly, still,
   I wanted to be wanted. Despite—to spite—
      that awkward, aborted shame, that touch

that spat in its eager taking, told me:
   *You are a piece of flesh
      for me to rub against, a corpse-*

still doll to climb on top of. Movement returned clumsily,
   foal-like and fumbling. Slowly, I kindled, broke into
      dailiness again, a traveler on unfamiliar turf.

A stone had grown in the fruit of my gut, slick and hard,
   a knowing. Or its opposite. But matter lacked
      for mattering around us, pinballs

bumping on the carnival of that porch, its loving sag
        into the street. You rooted me out, the fish hook
            of your smile snagging.

The way we both held our bodies back then: like collateral.
        You shouldn't have to share a syntax, a tongue,
            a summering with that trespass.

Dear one, fractured incandescence. You were angry for me
        before I could be. Thank you. We marked
            more than a year together

when I heard of his latest exploits, gut-punch glad
        his name sat somewhere in a file, that it could mean
            the others might be believed.

Here, he doesn't earn a name. Brute who never entered me,
        yet haunted for so long. He's rendered mute in the language
            of my my moving on. A body with no bell to ring,

                      rotting six feet under.

After Seeing *Black Swan* at Fifteen

Natalie Portman teaches me how to touch
        myself. Her body writhing in the bathtub,
hips arcing off the big screen: an offering.
        For years, I will rub only over the lace of my panties,
the warmdark of me too intimate even for my own fingers.
        I was perfect, she whispers in the final act,
blood blooming against the white of her feathered bodice.
Another girlish corpse hurtling deathward. At church,
        I pray for God to make me clean and count the minutes
until I can shroud myself in bedsheet and dance
into the sweat-ringed arms of sleep. The last and only person
        to see my budding body naked took a scalpel to it
(and how am I to know, years later, a lover will use the scar
as a road map? Lick the salt from its seam?). Pleasure, for me,
        has always come pricked with the embroidery of shame.
I take my right hand and deliver myself   from evil
into the sleek 'S' of a swan. This myth doesn't end
        how you think it will.
Not in flight   not in birth   but in song.

Her

after Kiki Smith

you will know me
    by this nakedness dun brushing against breast
a fuzzed tongue will pacify itself neck bending back
a reed bowed by wind   & who will be blamed, later
    and why
hunger me mother me suckle and bite
milk-warm   and sour in the cheek
  as midmorning sex listen the light leaks
from me   yes   something like
    a confession
wanted for a moment   to crawl inside her pelt
to re-womb   to be a soft wild   thing again
instead an offering   is this what you wanted
the two of us entombed by desire her neck snapped
a struck match
    when you see the creature wearing your old skin
      you will know her

Post-Surgical Ode

Suddenly, then, unburdened—
the muscles do not know the way
of ease. Sometimes fixing means taking
something out and sometimes it means
putting something in. The scar the same
bright slash either way. I stew under skin,
bones bump and shift. No more the nervy shriek
of shoulder, the taut warm knots of tendon.
These have loosened into pools of light, languid,
then storming towards new shapes. I stretch and flex,
let dust settle in the cracks of me. Blossom into poses
long untouched. The body a neglected toy
turned velveteen. I lounge. I stumble. I ark.
Inside me a menagerie. Zoo of lung and stubborn tissue.
What was planted there by blue-gloved hands, sprouting,
then sprouted. Later: scrubbed clean and stripped of screws,
I relearn each fret of spine. Press a finger to the seam.
They stitched me up nice and new. What is it—to look
in the mirror, turning and turning, and think, finally,
I could live here, yes—I live here. This slip of skin,
this jungle gym. Still off-kilter, sore with aftermath
and echo, this body always a negotiation. But mine
and uninterrupted. An unspooling:
the tender garden of my ribs in bloom. I reap the harvest daily.
My body is a bounty. I've paid. Today, I burst
each seed beneath my tongue. Even the sting of chapped flesh
something holy. I think of men in movies and their beloved,
beat-up cars. The goofy grin as they slap the hood, laugh—
She gets me where I'm going. Oh, you old girl.
You unthanked junk. You have taken me everywhere
I have asked you to go.

Diagnostic Notes on *The Bachelorette*

reality, sugar-spun,   the too-white teeth   of each
contestant clicking   like the pop of Orbit gum out of the pack.
for three months I've found myself   devouring,   gaze pinned
on their economy of vulnerability: *are you here
for the right reasons?* do you know how to play the game?

i admit, i was cynical at the beginning of *this journey.*
thought *The Bachelorette* could *never* be for me.
then the moon is out again.   the sliver in my chest waxes
& bloats. an emptiness   swells more space than it should.
yes, love, your absence fills me:

a sugarcane nausea.   a tug in the throat.   a waiting.
but enough about me. so what, i was a skeptic? you have to trust
the process: the careful giving over of the self.   the tender pit
of small talk. Becca sits in front of a man
who tells her he is his mother's only surviving child,
the other two dead (a few years apart) of overdose. we first kissed

a few weeks after your last bad relapse.
but it isn't this i think of first, it's my nervousness
as you turned each pill bottle in your hands   barechested,
the milkspilt moon silvering my twin bed into halves
& didn't ask. just waited   until it unspooled. that year of sharp
& shiver.   that was when i knew.

later, you will bandage the scars you kissed. it's a risk to strip
so early. to show your hand. how good or bad. how it shakes.
after champagne   & a dinner date,
Becca sends the suitor home. Something about spark
or lack of it or maybe   following her heart.
but through the canned rejection & recycled mantras, i find myself,

still   always   rooting for love, smiling into curled fingers
as someone else spills their guts   & hopes they stick.

How to Honeymoon in a Glass House

after Anne Carson's "The Glass Essay."

Nude #1:
Even bird-limbed and plaid-skirted, I shivered with want.
Each vertebra a genesis of crisis, body hissing Hallelujah
        warped as wire, hands grasping for something to scar.
I have never been good. I have only wrestled with the myth
        of my innocence until it quiets.

Nude #2:
This riot of flesh swarmed in sweat. September sinking its hull
        into the bank of autumn, summer swallowed
in a cool paste of sand and silt. These sweat lodge weeks seduce.
Their unintentional purity—
        everything spent and shimmering.

Nude #3:
The weight of you on top of me, grounding me,
        settling warm and heavy in the pit of my stomach.
Dreams of bloodied seafoam leave my sheets salt-starched.
I imagine a divorce from genealogy: curled in an oyster shell,
        born of myself. An act of unadulterated creation.

Nude #4:
Crabapples gored on macadam perfume the night with postpartum
as we walk home. You ask me what I want and my eyes skate
        blank, the reel of my iris catches and blurs
like the rolling credits of the films that soundtrack our sleep.
The question fishes a sharpness from my chest, brackish and slick.

Nude #5:
In a garage several states away, back braces tower like ruins:
      beheaded, whalebone white, and straining.
O holy relic, O sweat-stained fossil. You tell me if you could
have any name, you would go without. This is wise.
      Render love anonymous and it becomes without risk.

Nude #6:
While fucking, we mark the spots on each other's bodies
that have been punctured by IV
      with gentle fingertips, tongues thrusting
in clumsy mouths. You recognize my terror
of tenderness is at once a choked desire. Each time you cook steak,

      you leave it bloodier and I am learning to savor the slice
        of my incisors through fat.

On Asking for Directions Home

"Every landscape is autobiographical."—Alison Prine

Landscape 1

Struggle of zipper, hook, and snap—agony of air.
It's like licking a refrigerator, she says, as breath turns
crystalline. Sun plays in honeyed slats across the snow.
We crunch over powdered bone.

Then the rugged jewel spill
of Texas Falls, crags of jade polished slick
with riverflow. I want to wear it, this stark season.
Let the ice melt, then pool, in the hollow of my throat.

Half-thawed again, the embroidered thread
of highway stitches through burlap hills.
The cool car window pressed to my temple—
one final, insistent reminder.

Landscape 2

The brutal punch of wind
scrambles the words in my cheek. Slick broken teeth.
She fumbles with a lighter. I wonder how you're staying warm—
boiling pan of packed basement, laughter on a Saturday night,
the empty bottles singing by your window?

We walk back along the lakeshore, faces novocaine numb.
A man in a blue jacket tells us he is looking for a stray cat
to give her something to keep the cold out.

I think of my useless swaddling of fleece and wool.
The way January burrows through our tin ceilings,
ice splintering under the windowsill in spiderwebs.
The cold always gets in.

Landscape 3

We shove the bloom of our bodies
into the air as an offering, anyway.
The streets bleach chalk white.

I excavate their secrets with bitten fingernails
and bring my findings back to show you—
Look, here is the ellipse of wheat field that is my childhood,
here the crook of mountains snagging in my chest,
here the parched neon streets that croon hope, hope.

Backstroke with Lightning

The rocks sunned a Rothko red, edges scabbed and slick
with moss, I am debating the benefits of becoming
more mysterious.

The tin sheet of afternoon wavers against the shoreline,
the lake churning in thick slabs of slate,
cradling us back toward the rocks.

Daily I obliterate myself, leave prayer flag scraps waving
on the spikes of late-night conversations.
I want to learn a way of existing
that isn't as an open wound.

We dive under on a count of three, hair suspended in seaweed
tangles. I could live here, in this wild in-between.

Light tessellates over the lake floor,
a net of sun buoying us back toward being.
We emerge breathless, laughing, baptized.
Inhale the ripple of thunder, lightning metallic on my tongue.

Retreating to shore, I watch the storm descend without apology,
puckering the silk of the sand.
This is a necessary letting go. Here, watch me skin myself whole
and let the lake lick the pink of me clean.

Aubade for Vermont with Concussion

Slick of black ice. Skull sang asphalt & blood.
The heavy cotton of winter,
pressing on the backs of my eyes.
That lack was its own shade, winnowing me bare
& necessary, a bone picked clean.

I was unbuckled into spring.
Skin cracked with crocus, feverfew.
Memory as a residue: seltzer gone flat on the tongue,
      the smell of baking pavement,
the weave of worn carpet
branding our bare thighs through summer.
On Grant Street, those strange fruits would drop, split open,
everything sweet-rotten with their pulp.

Now, the season misbehaves by degrees.
My vision all pock & blur,
the blood leeched from the scene.
What else do I have to kill
to make it mine?

Unmaking

A confession: Some days, pain
struck me giddy. Bright spear. Beautiful uselessness.
Its logic unutterable, viscous.
No words I know   say the hotness—the entirety
of it. You know   last year I went half-mad,
grazing, smoke-dazed,
from one day to the next. Little bee.
> The blood baying at the seat of the spine, fevering me
> heavy. Animal unmade. The pelts of wolves reaped
> silver for longer than I'll likely live. We'd all like to leave
> a corpse worth something. Once, a cat left a furred husk
> at my feet and I mistook it   for a toy, the tiny ghost.
> All this to say: the body   separated
into pieces   becomes meat.
> When adopting a pet, they ask *Have you ever abandoned*
> *an animal? Have you ever had an animal lost or stolen?*
> I am jealous of the way animals live in the body,
> each motion patterned and parceled out. A unity
> I once grieved my lack of.
I am more wonder   than fear,
these days, but still partly girl:
in love with the bright jewel of the sky,
unable to fit words to what I want.
The cats' eyes cut like bulbs
though the dark. Some things, then,
are perfectly designed. It makes you crave
a god to believe in. When I ached, I was inscribed.
A story told enough times becomes scripture.
Now, I am careful what I worship.

Your grandmother says over Thanksgiving:
*We are called to repair what we can
of the world. Tikkun olam.*
        The words—the faith—not mine,
        but a credo I can cling to.
To live each day is dangerous, is sweet.
Wine souring in the cheek.
I no longer   believe
my body   will be saved.

Crushed Peaches

1.

The first time, you peel the dress from me
with practiced hands,
trace the ghost of an incision
from the nape of my neck
to where it pools in a hollow above my ass.
You do not look away.

2.

The night you're admitted,
I sleep in a chair,
buckled in the blunt posture of crisis.

Trace sigils on the backs of your hands,
kiss the creases of your elbows, sticky like crushed peaches.

I call my therapist from a public bathroom,
ask her what I've done wrong.
This is not about you, she says.

Later, I curl at your feet like a dog, dopey and adoring.
Cannula and cord tangle around us.
Your cannibal lungs gurgle and you spit blood.
I do not look away.

Interrogation After Flooding in Ellicot City

I am kin with every city built below sea level,
roads ruptured and storefronts mangled each time
rain swells the belly of the river and vomits its mud-sick silt.

Red tributary of burst vessel, inflammation of the everyday
pitched apocalyptic. I was born with famine in my blood,
a song of self-deprivation my infant flesh fever-hummed.

My body has always been a place for leaving. A burning building.
A valley glutted with the Patapsco River. After clearing remnants,
they will rebuild. Mine is a stupid kind of bravery—

the kind that makes a home in the wreckage.
Like living in a briar patch, needled with the memory
of your own mutilation. In the aftermath, critics hawk:

why repair? The floodplain stews with hostility.
Geography guarantees future disaster. We live
with the buzz of danger on the backs of our necks,

cross our fingers, learn to pray again, light a candle, build a levee.
Offerings to the homes that threaten to swallow us whole
and spit our bones out to rattle in the riverbed.

There is no higher ground. Even at my most gutted,
my skin clammy with scale rot, I dug a hook in the gaping mouth
of my calamity and refused evacuation.

On Self-Preservation

The instinct to preserve what we love   most is not unique.
My summer Polaroids   pressed flowers   unoriginal
in their simple joy. Some fossils are more accidental.
Things I never meant to carry   with me.

(In peat bogs across Northern Europe, they excavate ancient
corpses with strings of hair and flesh clinging to skeleton. One
girl's braid still intact, dyed a tannic red from centuries soaking in
acid swill).

I've always been a pack rat. Refused to part with what was done.
I am a lover   of little treasures: souvenir pins, pebbles polished
smooth and round, glossy postcards. Anything to say:
I've been here.

The lake I would walk to late at night, telling no one as I left.
Once, I believed I could be desired   only in my absence.

I reveled in being unaccounted for in the hours before dawn.
Jet black hazing to blue as the Adirondacks emerged
like approaching ships.

(Water here is particularly kind to wrecks. Entire steamers sit
pristine at thirty feet deep. War boats, too, decaying with all the
lush beauty of the lake-floor).

On bad nights, I would imagine the soft embrace of algae,
the slow   undressing   of the body by the elements.

Now I think the little animal living in my chest would fight
such an easy release. Even when I've kicked its ribs in, left
its fur matted with blood, the thing still wants so badly
just   to breathe.

Casualty

In 2016, 22,938 people committed suicide by firearm, while 14,415 people died in gun related homicides (NCHS, National Vital Statistics System, Mortality).

You survive yourself
to find your body is a weapon

detonated. Your helix a fuse,
blood a singing gun.

A deer paints its brains
across glass. *It happens all the time,*

my father says after a near miss,
our valley overrun with them.

Nearby, children rehearse their own murder,
crouching in closets full of glue.

We name this an anomaly
so not to rob ourselves of sleep.

Outlast a death wish, and the day opens
in daisies, crows, carrion. Oh, the bright shock

of it, flush against the future's throat:
a cocked gun. Meanwhile,

 some men in a boardroom say bullets are no threat.
After all, most deaths are delivered

by the same hand that falls limp, then cooling,
in the knot of aftermath. Show me a story

not hedged against its ending. Show me
the warped hull of my ship, waterlogged and stubborn,

sailing for some silent coast. There, I will live
monarchical, fatten on a diet of brocade.

The softest thing to ever fall so hard
and splendid. Come fresh from some hurt, stinging.

You survive the body
to find the self a spent shell, glittering.

Meditations on Disaster

Heat-struck and hazy, the pulse pooled in the skull. A tide shimmers, it seeks. To harbinge is a heavy-tongued gift. The kind that gets caught in the teeth. That Cassandra was right, in the end, did not matter.

*

I practice prophecy like arpeggio, scales of what-if flaking. Catalog of disaster: bridge, cliff, car, plane, fire, quake, flood. As a child, I collected stones, aventurine jumbled with river-rock and gravel. Imbued them with clumsy spells, the ones all children know. No proof of their luck but my feet still planted.

*

Remember the story? The woman, love-hewn, slowly swallows herself in stone, skin slanting granite, teeth glistening. There's some truth to that transformation. I clutch the love I've been given like a purse full of blood. It stains. Sustains. Listen, anything can be taken away and will be. One day I will kiss the mossy lips of Blarney. One day the ones who keep me in my skin will cleave away. Certain faults reveal themselves, map the earth's wrestled glacial gain. I tried to study their branching, divine the future from that geologic past. Instead, I slipped backwards, untongued.

*

The past isn't static. It hops and shocks, skips through me like a virus. It snores, sleep-dumb and dormant, waiting. Cicada hum under concrete. The sweet gum tree I screwed my gaze on when I knew my grandmother would die, that all those tubes and mutterings meant an ending. She still lives in peppermint, the cloy of bergamot. A splinter, glinting.

*

When I go, I want to taste like champagne and ocean. Brackish and sweet all at once. Let me cling here with the same fierceness I latch to my lover, refusing erosion. I will not be swallowed, but spit. Going out with the salt hum of the tide, licking every shell and pebble goodnight, goodnight, goodnight. Dear ones, I am not ready to let go, will never be, completely—
what luck.

Voicemail with Shipwreck

soon a lakelessness   a lack
will stitch through each day   silvery ache of   unhome
will you stay   with me   then when   my skull is cotton-
stuffed   and throbbing   minnowing for that
      Adirondack churn
when I crave the lake like   a smoke   want to inhale algae
      deep into alveoli
          then deeper—

last summer a boy my sibling's age   drowned   swimming out
past the buoys   *well no two swims are the same*   how to
explain to you why this makes me cry   for half an hour
though I didn't know him   it's not that I believe this landscape
        saved me   but it anchored   if you look
its striations settle in my skin   curl around hip bone
and belly   this leviathan
claiming another wreck   as its own.

sirening myself
    my own rock   -sharp shore   mast-lashed
wrists straining   then slack.

I need to know you   will swim with me   will you stay
      with my unmooring   if not for mystery   then
for the familiar stroke   of skin against skin
for the something   like a lake   like an ocean
we stretch   tenderly between us.

The Last Known Living Speaker's Survival Manual

I am replete with unkindness,
branches sprouting from my back,
brambles clinging to my fur. The crows
are frozen mid-flight, wings outstretched,
talons still tangled in the thicket of me.
I have given myself up to a language
you can never be native to.

My hair grows rank, underbrush threatening
to swallow my milk-face whole. Even now,
the roots have spread, buds erupting from my chest,
their little green lips pursed in pleasure.
I have always hurt so selfishly—

I am thinking of the vines flossing through my teeth,
spilling over my lips in a parody of sickness.
Of the way something red and jagged unfurled in me
on seeing the smooth white scars on a stranger's arm,
little tally marks of some private accounting.

Everyday a language collapses into silence
and my body devours itself in dragon's mouth
and dogwood. I am the kind of wilderness
they used to call unforgiving.

I think I am learning to be kind. This, too, is a type of survival.

Communion

"There are knives that glitter like altars."—Charles Simic

Each Sunday, I would bring the cold lip of the chalice
to my mouth, swallowing only air.
We learn early to approximate the holiness
we cannot capture.

And always there was the question of what to do
with the loneliness of my wrists—lily-white and barren
as the altar before Easter. This took longer to learn.

The first time, the blood pearled along the vein like stigmata,
each thin line erupting into raised red braille.

Not a prayer but an attempt at alchemy.
Even the Holy Ghost marveled at my knack
for the miraculous. I took each rotten rib
and wrenched it out. Injury as a mode of transfiguration—
turning static into something sharp and starved.

Pain demands
a form to cling to—a crucifix, a mother tongue, a scar.
When the marks first began to fade,
I mourned them, each dash a stillbirth nestled in my gut.

I tilt the cup to my lips without thinking now,
mouth fuzzed with Christ-blood.
I am still trying to unbend the glittering altar of my body
into something livable. In the future I will be shaped
like something I can forgive.

Lambflesh

i want to paint my skin with sun   crack the day open so its easter egg guts spill out. maybe then i can be illuminated. drag of knuckles across brick. say: here, like this. snap of rubber band against lambflesh of inner wrist. i am a difficult thing to love but i want you to try anyway. to be known is a risk i cannot afford. revenge fantasy pt. 1: to be holy, to be whole as a vessel. the mud of my viscera spooled so tight i no longer inhabit the space after deluge. revenge fantasy pt. 2: to be understood so completely i can shed the barbed wire borders of my body, the strangle of snakeskin silence for   something else   something new.   i have outlived many incarnations but there is still   always the tarred and feathered insistence of memory. the tally of leaving, the way she couldn't meet my eyes as we stood barefoot in the parking lot.

i dreamed your hand brushed mine and our fingers laced like fishing net. i dreamed a woman slept and you sliced her face off. i want you to love me when i am tender and   beaten bloody but
              i can't bear to be tender.

i roll over. i play dead. i get up again.

About the Author

Caroline Shea is a writer and an MFA candidate in poetry at New York University. She is also an editor at Green Writers Press, a small New England publisher with a focus on sustainability. Her work has appeared in Crab Fat Magazine, The Pinch, and Tinderbox Poetry Journal, among other publications. Recently, she was the recipient of The Pinch Literary Award for poetry, as well as a finalist for the Brett Elizabeth Jenkins Poetry Prize.

More information about Caroline's writing can be found at https://caroline-fitzgerald-shea.squarespace.com.

www.ingramcontent.com/pod-product-compliance
Lightning Source LLC
Chambersburg PA
CBHW021027090426
42738CB00007B/930